PLUTO

For my mom, whose heart could
warm the entire solar system—KJ

For the two brightest stars in
my life, Sheryl and Isla—AJR

PENGUIN WORKSHOP
An Imprint of Penguin Random House LLC, New York

Text copyright © 2020 by Penguin Random House LLC. Illustrations copyright © 2020 by Andrew J. Ross. All rights reserved.
Published by Penguin Workshop, an imprint of Penguin Random House LLC, New York. PENGUIN and PENGUIN WORKSHOP are
trademarks of Penguin Books Ltd, and the W colophon is a registered trademark of Penguin Random House LLC. Manufactured in China.

Visit us online at www.penguinrandomhouse.com.

Library of Congress Cataloging-in-Publication Data is available upon request.

ISBN 9780593096291   10 9 8 7 6 5 4 3 2 1

HEART ON PLUTO

by Karl Jones • illustrated by Andrew J. Ross

Penguin Workshop

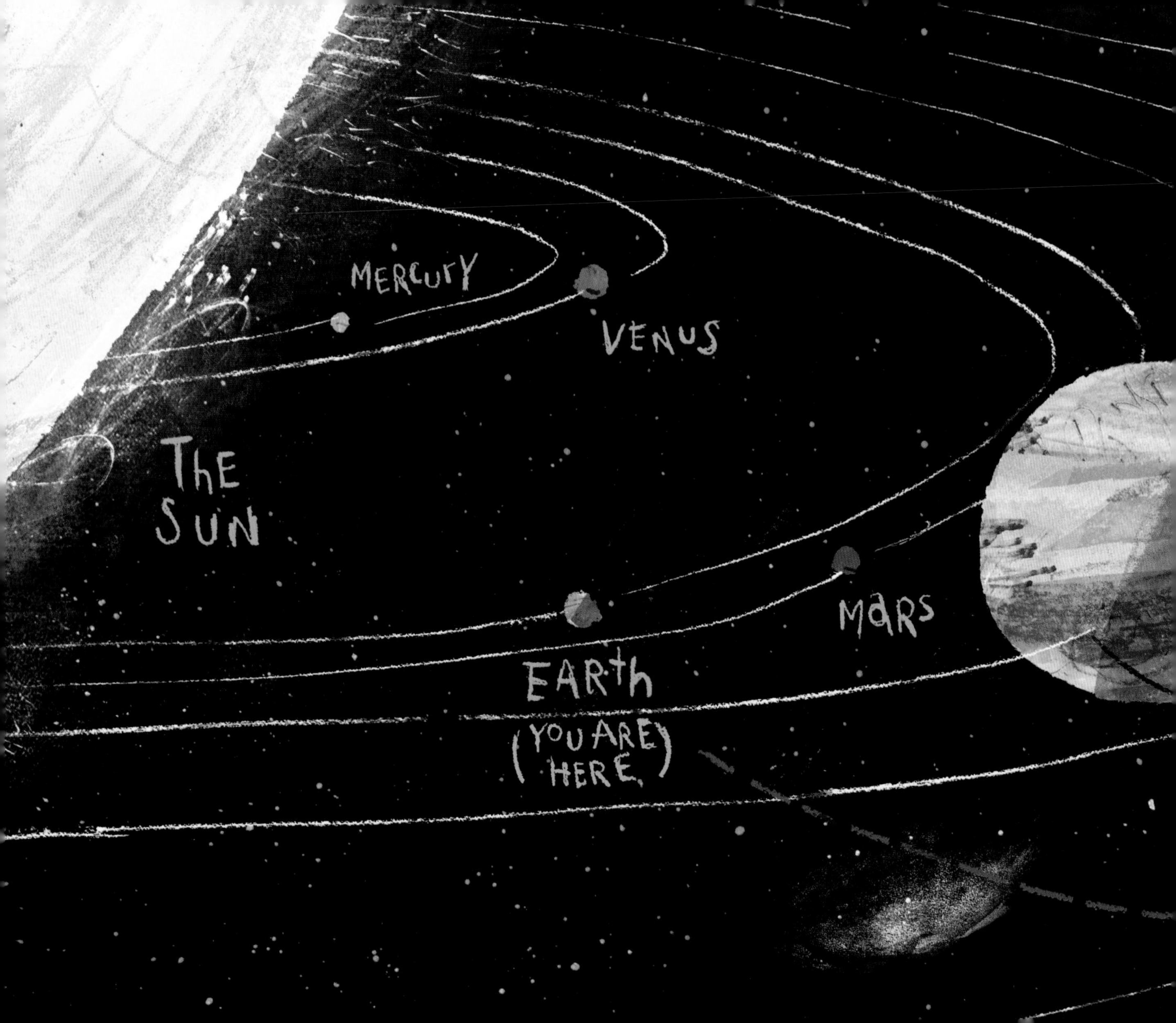
MERCURY
VENUS
THE SUN
MARS
EARTH
(YOU ARE HERE)

Hello, Solar System.

SatuRN

I AM
HERE!

JUPiTeR

URANUS

NepTuNe

PLuTo

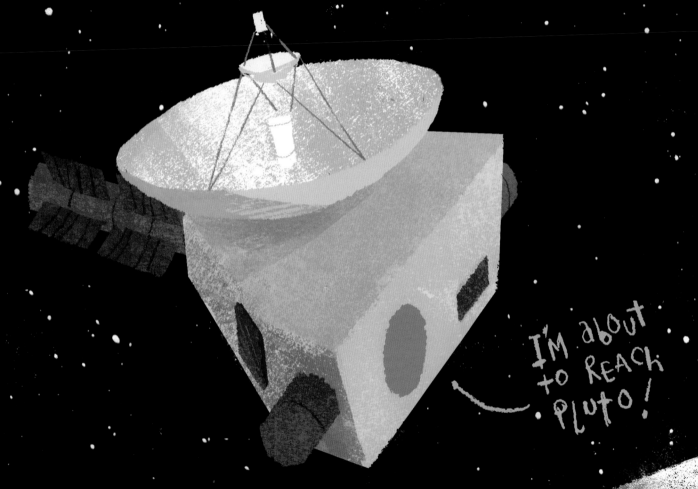

Today is a big day.

I'm about to REACH PLUTO!

My name is New Horizons.

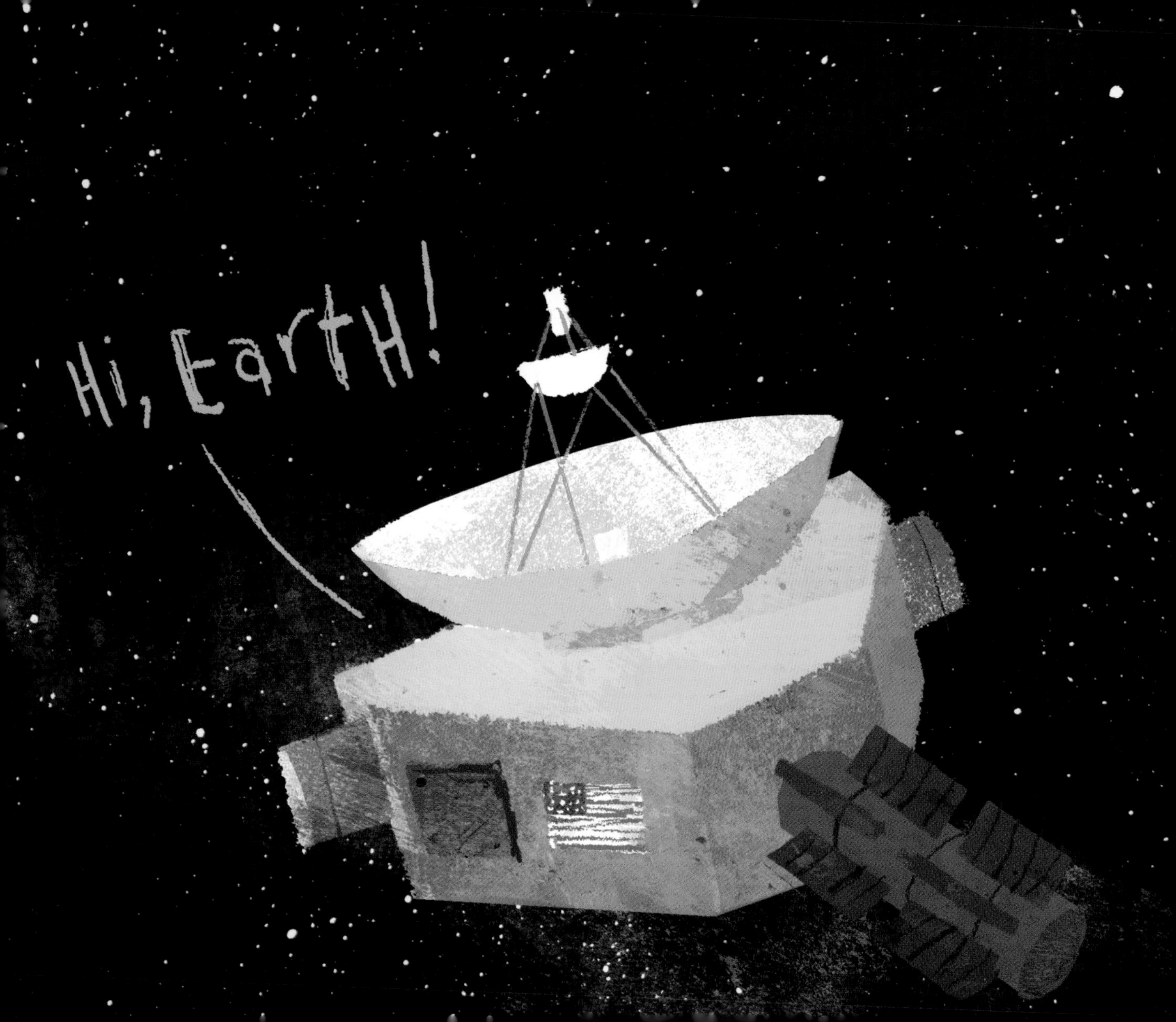
Hi, EartH!

That's Really FAR!
NEW HORIZONS
ATLAS
NASA
ILS AVO
LOCKHEED MARTIN
ILS
USAF

I have a big job to do here in space. I was sent from Earth to travel all the way to Pluto.

On my way, I traveled past the largest planet in our solar system, Jupiter. I took lots of pictures and sent them to my friends on Earth.

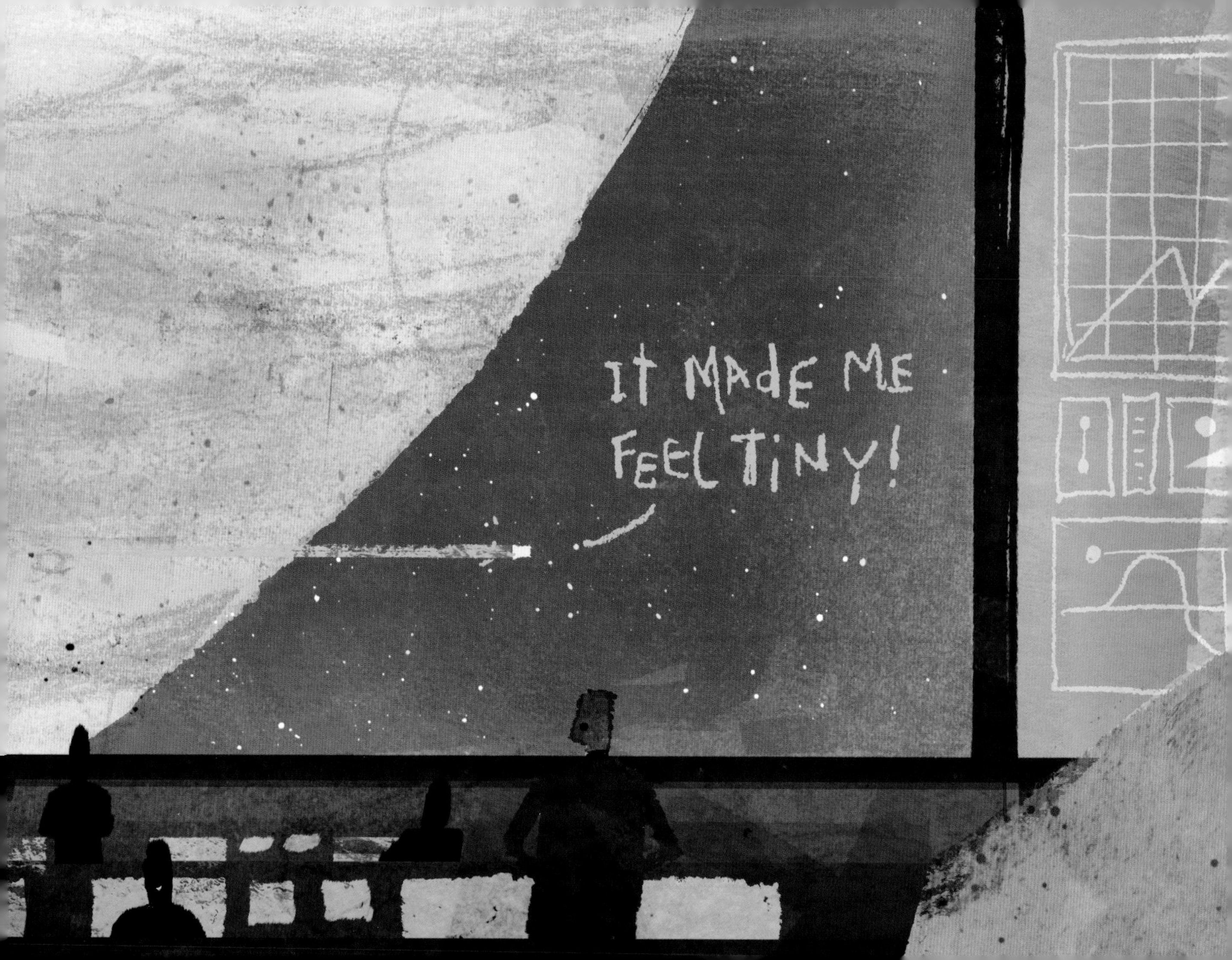
IT MADE ME
FEEL TINY!

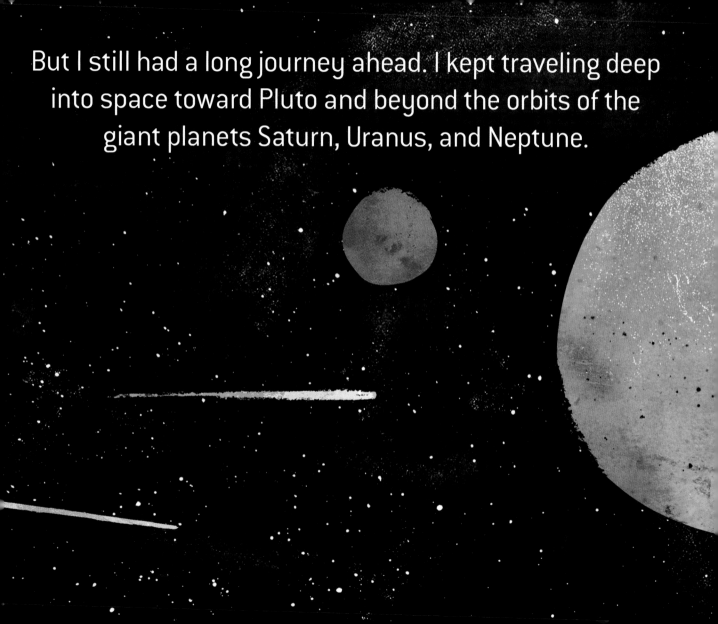

But I still had a long journey ahead. I kept traveling deep into space toward Pluto and beyond the orbits of the giant planets Saturn, Uranus, and Neptune.

Within our solar system, Pluto is one of the farthest objects from the sun. It's lonely out here. No human-made object (or human!) has ever been this close to Pluto before.

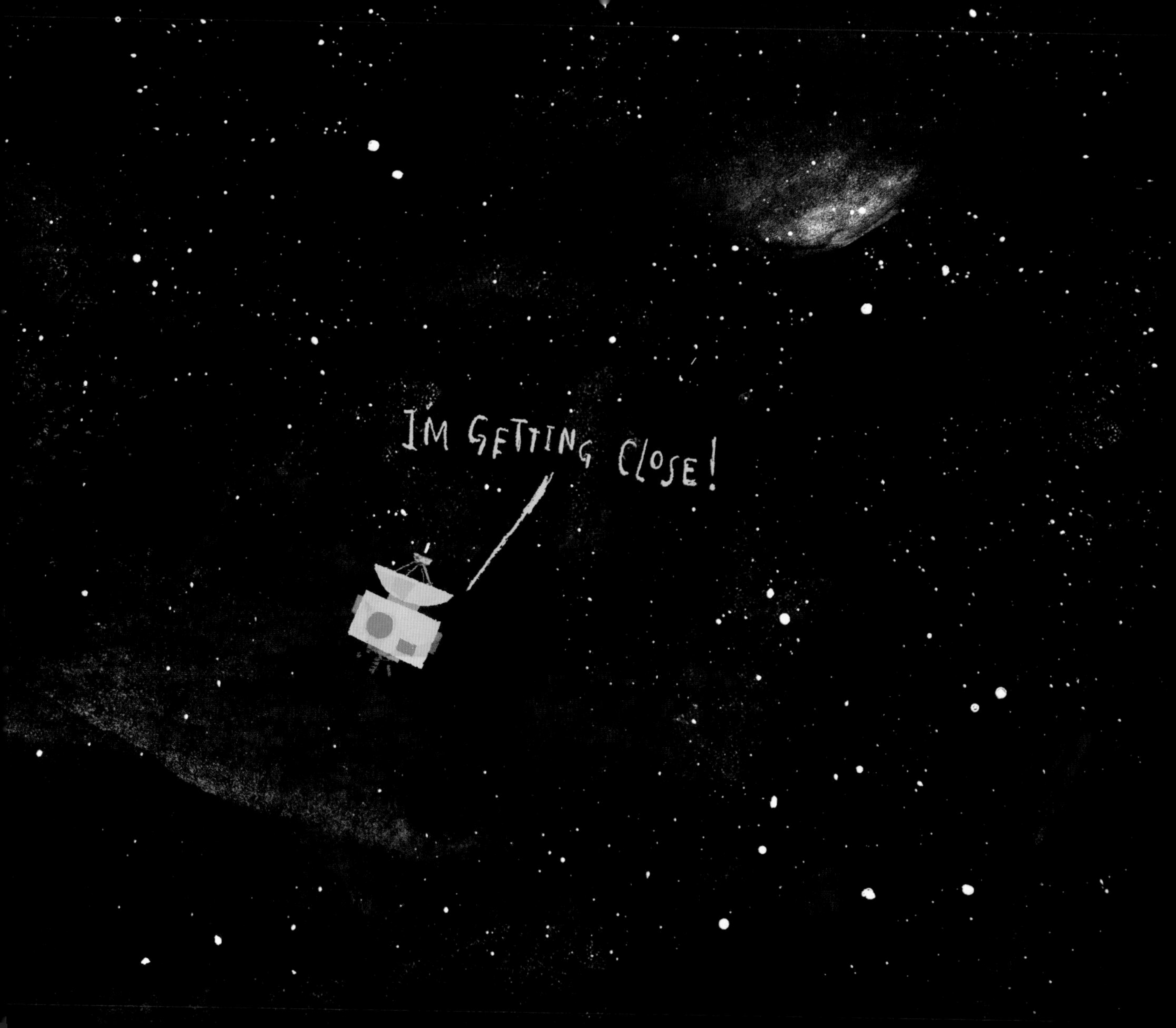
I'M GETTING CLOSE!

What we know about Pluto has changed a lot over time.
We used to call Pluto a planet.

But now scientists call it a dwarf planet, because it's so small.

We still study Pluto, because there is so much more to discover.

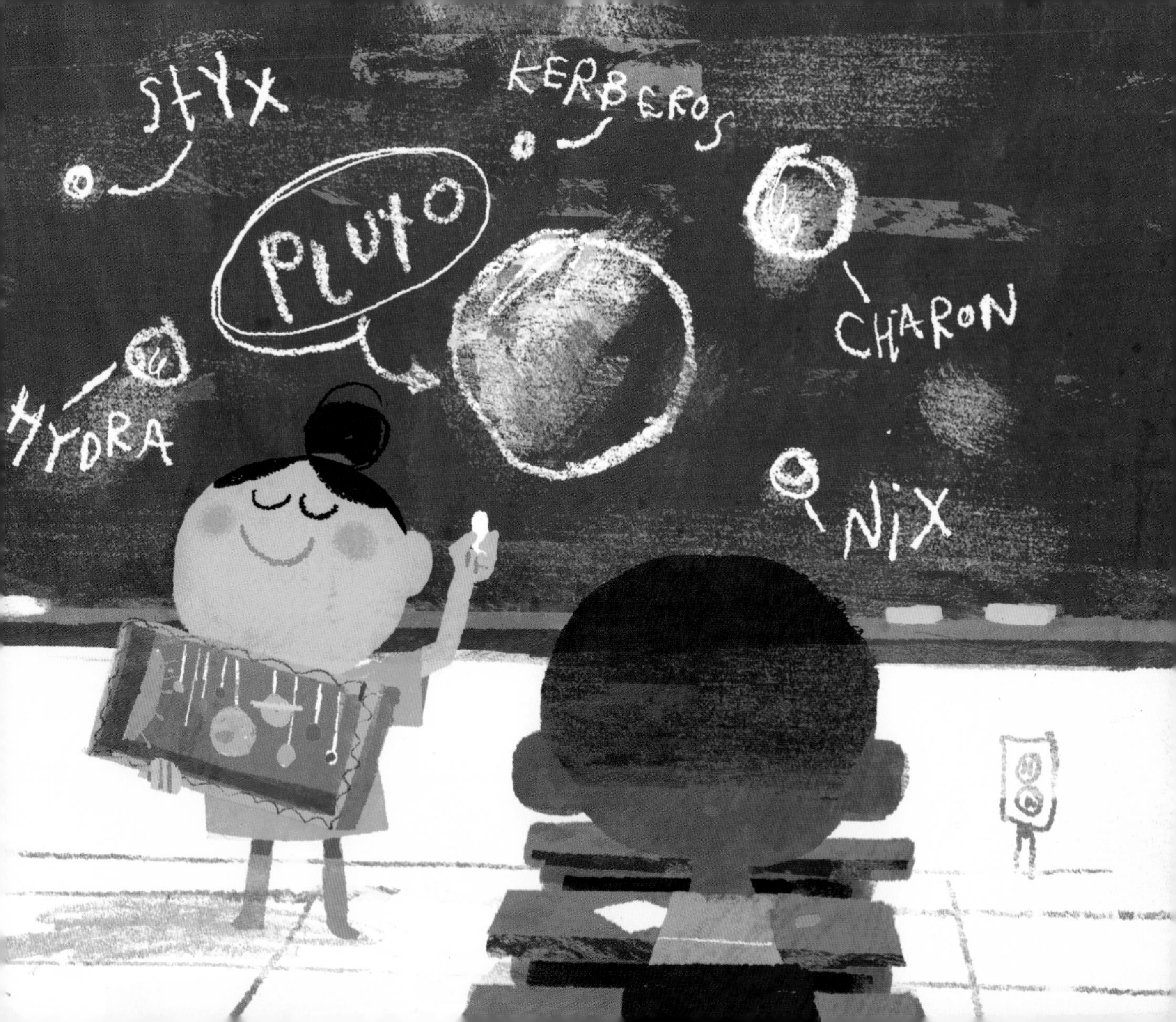
STYX
KERBEROS
PLUTO
CHARON
HYDRA
NIX

After nine long years, I arrived at my destination.